So You Think You Know Golf?

Who, What, Where, When and Why— Test Your Golf IQ!

So You Think You Know Golf?

Who, What, Where, When and Why— Test Your Golf IQ!

by Bill Kroen

PRICE STERN SLOAN
Los Angeles

Kroen, William C.
So you think you know golf?/Bill Kroen.
        p.   cm.
        ISBN 0-8431-3432-1
        1. Golf—Miscellanea. I. Title.
GV965747   1992
796.352—dc20   92-16127
                                    CIP

NOTICE: The information contained in this book is true and complete to the best of our knowledge. All recommendations are made without any guarantees on the part of the author or of Price Stern Sloan, Inc. The author and publisher disclaim all liability in connection with the use of this information.

This book has been printed on acid-free paper.

ACKNOWLEDGEMENTS

I wish to thank Bruce Hoster of Dunlop Sports, Bill Carnes and Tom Tehan for their invaluable help. Also, Diane Becker of the USGA provided me with a great deal of assistance and my special thanks go out to her and that wonderful organization.

I also realize how fortunate I am to have the talent and expertise of an editor such as Corrine Johnson of PSS.

DEDICATION

To my daughter Kerry, who has given us all a lesson in courage.

TABLE OF CONTENTS

1

"The Best Game At Which to Be Bad"

Golf

1. What are the odds of making a hole-in-one for the average golfer?
    a. 500 to 1
    b. 4,350 to 1
    c. 8,404 to 1
    d. 15,300 to 1

2. What is an "albatross" in golf?

3. What was the name of the first golf ball produced by Spalding?

4. In the early days of golf, what was a "gutty"?

5. Where is the World Golf Hall of Fame located?
    a. St. Andrews, Scotland
    b. Far Hills, New Jersey
    c. Augusta, Georgia
    d. Pinehurst, North Carolina

In a match, Reggie is 25 feet from the hole and just off of the green. His opponent, Jim, is on the green just three feet from the hole. Reggie putts to within one foot of the hole, walks up to his ball and taps it in. Jim claims that Reggie played out of turn. Ruling, please.

Reggie has played out of turn since he was not on the green for his first putt. Jim may ask him to replace the last putt and play it over.

---

6. True-False. After winning the Grand Slam, Bobby Jones never won another tournament.

So You Think You Know Golf?

7. What is a Texas Wedge?

8. What is the unofficial scorekeeper who follows a player in a tournament called?

9. Where did the word "tee" come from?

10. What percentage of golfers are left-handed?

11. What is the distance of the longest hole-in-one ever recorded?

12. What is the distance of the longest drive ever recorded in a long drive contest?
    a. 397 yards
    b. 437 yards
    c. 459 yards
    d. 502 yards

13. Who is called "The Father of American Golf"?

14. Who was the first president of the United States Golf Association?

15. What was the practice of blocking your opponent's ball with your ball called?

16. What is the longest hole in the world?

17. What does the British term "dragon's teeth" refer to?

18. The Atlanta National Golf Course has a life-sized statue of which of the following greats?
    a. Byron Nelson
    b. Bobby Jones
    c. Gene Sarazen
    d. Ben Hogan

19. Two pairs of father-sons have won the British Open. Name them.

20. What does the acronym GHIN on your handicap card stand for?

21. True-False. Architect Robert Trent Jones is Bobby Jones' first cousin.

Donna's ball lies in heavy thicket. As she sets up to the ball, swings back and starts her downswing, her club gets caught in the bushes before it reaches the ball. Is this a stroke?

Yes, this is a stroke because Donna did not "voluntarily" check her downswing.

22. How old must one be to be eligible for the United States Senior Amateur?

23. What is the most popular name for a country club in the United States?
    a. Riverside
    b. Meadowbrook
    c. Hillcrest
    d. Lakeside

24. True-False. Sam Snead, Ben Hogan and Byron Nelson were all born in the same year.

25. Who were known as "The Triumvirate" in golf lore?
    a. Palmer, Nicklaus and Player
    b. J.H. Taylor, Baird and Vardon
    c. Snead, Nelson and Hogan
    d. Ouimet, Vardon and Ray

26. In what golf shot, if executed properly, will the club never come in contact with the ball?

27. What is the term in golf for dangling the putter vertically in front of your eyes to determine the break of a putt?

28. What president had a putting green installed behind the White House?

    a. William Howard Taft
    b. Dwight Eisenhower
    c. Gerald Ford
    d. George Bush

29. In 1973, who made a hole-in-one in the British Open, 50 years after playing in his first one?

    a. John Morris
    b. Byron Nelson
    c. Gene Sarazen
    d. Sam Snead

30. Who was the first woman to win the USGA's Bob Jones' Award?

    a. Mickey Wright
    b. Patty Berg
    c. Babe Zaharias
    d. Joanne Carner

31. According to the USGA's guidelines, what are the recommended maximum distances for each of these holes: par 3, par 4 and par 5?

Tom chips from the edge of the green. The ball lodges between the pin and the edge of the hole. He walks over to the hole, pulls the fagstick out and causes the ball to pop straight up and come to rest on the green about two inches from the hole. Ruling, please.

There is no penalty but the ball has not been holed as yet. Tom must now putt the ball in and count the additional stroke.

32. What is a "flier"?

33. Where did the term "bogey" come from?

34. What is the term for a player with a 0 handicap?

35. How many rules are there in the Rules of Golf?
    a. 10
    b. 18
    c. 34
    d. 127

36. What is the system called that equalizes handicaps from course to course?

37. What is the name given to the rules-making meetings held between the USGA and the Royal and Ancient committees?

38. What is a "rub of the green" in golf?

39. Why do the Rules of Golf prohibit grounding of clubs in a hazard?

40. What is "making a snowman" in golf?

41. What are "tiger tees"?

42. What is a "sandbagger" in golf?

43. How much money is spent or generated by golf in the United States in one year?
    a. 28 million dollars
    b. 128 million dollars
    c. 20 billion dollars
    d. 30 billion dollars

44. What golf scoring system uses a point value for scores on each hole instead of total strokes?

45. What is a "dot" in golf?

46. Who was the first American born player to win the British Open?

47. The USGA prohibits "Calcuttas." What is a Calcutta?

48. True-False. There are more private courses than public courses in America.

49. What is a "sandy"?

50. In 1457, King James II banned golf in Scotland. Why?

Kristen's ball is plugged in a sand trap. She walks over to a nearby trap, takes a swing and lets her club pass through the sand. She then returns to the trap where her ball lies and plays a successful shot onto the green. Is this legal?

This is a violation of Rule 13-4, which prohibits the testing of the consistency of sand in a hazard or similar hazard. In match play, it is a loss of the hole. In medal it is a two-stroke penalty.

"The Best Game At Which to to Be Bad"

Golf

1. The average golfer has an 8,404 to 1 chance of making a hole-in-one.

2. An "albatross" is a name given to a double eagle or three under par on one hole.

3. the Spalding Wizard

4. a ball made from gutta-percha

5. d. Pinehurst, North Carolina

6. True. He retired.

7. using a putter from off of the green

8. a "marker"

9. The Scottish word "teay" meaning "a pile of sand."

10. 5.5%

11. The record for the longest hole in one on a straight hole is 447 yards by Robert Mitera. L. Bruce made a 480 yard hole-in-one on a dog-leg hole.

12. b. Jack L. Hamm used his "Jackhammer" driver to belt a drive 437 yards in 1989.

13. John Reid

14. Theodore Havermeyer

15. a stymie

16. The longest hole in the world is the 7th hole (par 7) of the Sano Course, Satuki GC, Japan, which measures 909 yards, according to *The Guinness Book of World Records*.

17. Dragon's teeth is unmowed grass in a bunker.

18. c. Gene Sarazen

19. Old Tom Morris and Young Tom Morris along with Willie Park Senior and Junior.

20. Golf Handicap Information Network

21. False. They are of no relation.

22. 55

23. c. Hillcrest

24. True. They were all born in 1902.

25. b. J.H. Taylor, Baird and Vardon

26. The sand shot. The club slides under the ball and through the sand without touching the ball.

27. plumb-bobbing

28. b. Dwight Eisenhower had a green built to work on his putting.

29. c. Gene Sarazen

30. c. Babe Zaharias

31. par 3—Up to 250 yards
    par 4—Up to 470 yards
    par 5—470 on up

32. A flier is a ball that flies with little or no spin. The flier is often caused by grass or water covering the grooves on the clubface.

33. At the Royal Yarmouth Golf Club, members referred to an imaginary member named Colonel Bogey who always shot par. The term changed to meaning one over par when the game came to America.

34. a scratch player

35. c. 34

36. the Slope System

37. the Quadrennial Conferences

38. A "rub of the green" occurs when a ball is moved or deflected by an outside agency. For example, a ball headed toward the green strikes a bird in flight. It's a term for a twist of fate.

39. The rules prohibit grounding or placing the club on the ground in a hazard because the hazard is specifically designated a penalty situation for a bad shot. The grounding of clubs might alter the lie or give the player added information on the texture of the sand, soil or mud in which the ball lies.

40. making a score of 8 on one hole

41. Tiger tees are those that are placed as far back on the hole as possible.

42. A "sandbagger" is a player who misrepresents his true ability by carrying a higher handicap than he deserves.

43. c. 20 billion dollars. This amount spent on golf in the United States, includes real estate monies as well.

44. Stableford

45. A "dot" occurs when a player's tee shot on a par three lands closest to the hole among his/her foursome.

46. Walter Hagen

47. A Calcutta is an auction during which individuals bid on players or teams. The highest bidder owns the player or team for an event and wins from the pool of money, if the player or team wins in competition.

48. False. There are more courses open to the public.

49. A "sandy" is getting the ball out of a sand trap then one putting.

50. He felt that golf was undermining military training and discipline.

2

FROM "CALAMITY JANE" TO "BIG BERTHA"

THE EQUIPMENT

1. Who invented the sand wedge?

2. What is the name that Mizuno has given to its line of ladies' clubs?

3. What are the five criteria a golf ball must adhere to in order to pass USGA regulations?

4. What company was the first to offer titanium shafts in its line?
   a. Cobra
   b. Taylor Made
   c. Mizuno
   d. Lynx

5. True-False. A club may have a design that allows for an adjustment in the weight of the club.

6. What kind of wood is usually used in laminated woods?
   a. maple
   b. persimmon
   c. ash
   d. hickory

7. What was the name of the oversized putter used by Jack Nicklaus to win the 1986 Masters?

8. What company offered one million dollars to any touring professional who would use its ball to win a major tournament?

9. What does "MD" stand for on Maxfli's Tour Limited ball?

10. Name the famous golf equipment companies that are located in these cities:

    a. Fort Worth, TX
    b. Greenville, SC
    c. Louisville, KY
    d. Albany, GA
    e. Chicopee, MA

11. What is the principle or advantage of "offset" clubs?

12. True-False. There is no regulation as to the length of a club.

13. Why were early clubs sometimes called "spoons"?

14. What does "DTR" stand for on Titleist clubs?

15. What is the purpose of dimples on a golf ball?

In a medal tournament, a touring pro asks a member of the gallery what club the other pros were hitting to a par three hole that he is about to play. The gallery member does not know. Is there any penalty?

Rule 8-1 prohibits the asking for or giving of advice. There is a two-stroke penalty.

---

16. What is "gear effect" in regard to golf club construction?

17. What was the name of Karsten Solheim's first commercial putter?

18. Match the early club names to their present day counterparts.

    niblick   2 wood
    cleek   5 iron
    mid-iron   9 iron
    spoon   2 iron
    brassie   4 wood

19. In what year did the USGA set a 14 club limit?

    a. 1925
    b. 1938
    c. 1954
    d. 1960

So You Think You Know Golf?

20. What is the recommended height of a flagstick?
    a. 5 feet
    b. 6 feet
    c. 7 feet
    d. 8 feet

21. If swingweight of a club relates to its balance point, what is the name given to describe a club's total weight?

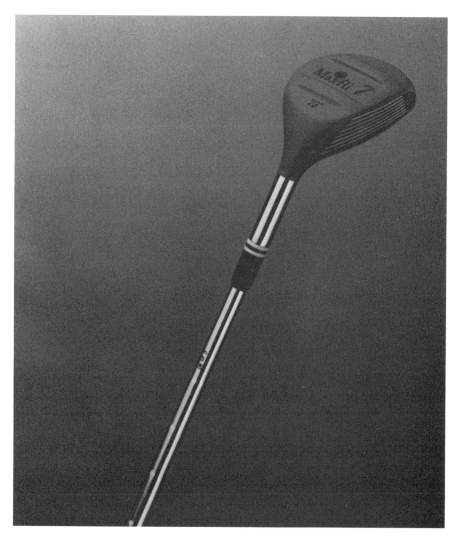

In a match, Paul's ball is on the green. When he cannot find a coin in his pocket, he decides to lay his sand wedge down and marks his ball at the tip of the grip. He lifts the ball, cleans it and replaces it in the exact spot where he has it marked with his sand wedge. His opponent asks for a ruling.

Paul has not violated any rule. The Rules of Golf do not specify what must be used as a ball marker.

22. What is the name of the plastic cap that fits over the joint between the shaft and the clubhead?

23. What is considered the standard loft of a driver?
    a. 9 degrees
    b. 11 degrees
    c. 12 degrees
    d. 14 degrees

24. What company once advertised that no one was paid to use its equipment?

25. With what equipment company was Arnold Palmer first associated?
    a. Spalding
    b. Dunlop
    c. Wilson
    d. Axiom

26. What two companies control about 40% of the golf-glove industry?

So You Think You Know Golf?

27. In what state are the golf shoe giants, Etonic and Footjoy, both located?

28. What does "DDH" stand for on Maxfli balls?

29. What was the name of Bobby Jones' putter?

30. What company sponsors the National Long Drive Contest?

31. In 1988, the Karsten Manufacturing Company waged a national advertising campaign and a lawsuit against the USGA over an equipment ruling. What was the nature of the dispute?

32. In 1987, MacGregor issued a set of 25th anniversary commemorative clubs to honor Jack Nicklaus. Appropriately, what was the cost of the set?

33. Lee Trevino switched from endorsing one automobile company to another in 1991. What were the companies?

34. In 1988, one golf ball manufacturer had three out of four winners of the majors—Curtis Strange (U.S. Open), Sandy Lyle (Masters) and Jeff Sluman (PGA). What ball was it?

    a. Titleist
    b. Maxfli
    c. Spalding
    d. Wilson

Sheila has a tap-in putt of only a few inches. She addresses the ball but as she starts her backswing, a gust of wind blows the ball into the cup. Ruling, please.

Since Sheila has addressed the ball and it has moved, she must replace the ball and putt with a one-stroke penalty added for a violation of Rule 18-2b.

On the day of the finals for the club championship, in a match play event, Kevin walks out to every hole to check the pin placements and stops to putt on some greens to test the speed. His opponent comes to you as Rules Chairman for a ruling.

Kevin is well within the rules. Practice on the course before a match play event is allowed.

35. Match these pros with the clubs that they endorse.

Greg Norman	Spalding
Tom Watson	Maxfli
Tom Kite	Ram
Jan Stephenson	Cobra
Lee Trevino	Hogan

36. What is the main characteristic that collectors prize in a set of persimmon woods?

37. What company was first to introduce irons that combined forged and cavity back design?

38. What was the name of the elongated putter that became popular on the Senior Tour?

39. What brand of grips do 95% of Tour players use?

40. What is the standard length of a driver?

41. What company came out with a set of clubs that were all the same in length? What were they called?

42. What company features golf balls that have different colored halves?

43. Name the putter that Sam Snead used that was later outlawed by the USGA.

44. At the beginning of the 17th century a perpetual peace treaty was signed between England and Scotland. How did this affect golf equipment?

45. What are "The Whale," "The Judge" and "Fat Eddie"?

46. When John Huston vaulted into the lead of the 1991 Honda Classic, his shoes were declared illegal. What were they? Why were they illegal?

47. What is the name of the survey company that keeps track of what brands the tournament players use in Tour events?

48. Many club manufacturers now use a material called Kelvar for their woods and irons. For what use was Kelvar first developed?

Bob's ball is in-bounds but lies next to an out-of-bounds stake. The stake interferes with Bob's backswing. He pulls the stake out, plays his shot then replaces the stake. Is this OK?

Bob cannot remove an out-of-bounds stake as it is not an obstruction under the Rules of Golf. This is a loss of hole or two-stroke penalty.

---

49. What company calls its club a "weapon"?

50. What company carries Bobby Jones' signature on its products?

FROM "CALAMITY JANE" TO "BIG BERTHA"

THE EQUIPMENT

1. Gene Sarazen

2. Miz

3. Weight—No greater than 1.620 ounces
   Size—No less than 1.680 inches in diameter
   Spherical symmetry
   Initial velocity—Not faster than 250 feet per second
   Overall Distance Standard

4. b. Taylor Made

5. True.

6. a. maple

7. The Response ZT

8. Bullet

9. Maximum Distance

10. a. Fort Worth, TX—Hogan

    b. Greenville, SC—Dunlop

    c. Louisville, KY—Powerbilt

    d. Albany, GA—MacGregor

    e. Chicopee, MA—Spalding

11. "Offset" clubs help the player keep his/her hands in front of the ball and make it easier to get the ball airborne.

12. False. Clubs must have a shaft of at least 18 inches.

13. The early clubs had concave faces that promoted a scooping type action—thus the name "spoon."

14. Distance Through Research

15. Dimples trap the air and cause the ball to lift into the air from the spin off of the club. The dimples also serve to stabilize the ball in flight.

16. On woods, there is a lateral bulge across the face of the club. This slight curvature causes balls struck off center (toward the heel or toe) to spin in a manner that brings the ball back toward the target.

17. Ping Anser

18. niblick   9 iron

    cleek   2 iron

    mid iron   5 iron

    spoon   4 wood

    brassie   2 wood

19. b. 1938

20. c. 7 feet

21. static weight

22. ferrule

23. c. 12 degrees

24. Titleist

25. c. Wilson

26. Footjoy and Titleist

27. Massachusetts

28. isododecahedron (it refers to a specialized dimple pattern)

29. Calamity Jane

30. Michelin Tire Company

31. The dispute was over Ping's squared grooves on their irons and whether or not they conformed to USGA specifications.

32. $2,500

33. Toyota to Cadillac

34. b. Maxfli

35.
Greg Norman	Cobra
Tom Watson	Ram
Tom Kite	Hogan
Jan Stephenson	Maxfli
Lee Trevino	Spalding

36. matching grain patterns in the woods

37. Hogan (Edge)

38. Slim Jim

39. Golf Pride

40. 43 inches

41. Tommy Armour (E.Q.L.)

42. Ping

43. croquet putter

44. Bow and arrow makers utilized their skills with wood and metal to make golf clubs as a means of staying in business.

45. oversized drivers

46. His Weight-Rite shoes, designed to force a player's weight toward the center for better balance, violated the "building a stance" rule. Incidentally, he went on to win the tournament.

47. Darrell

48. army helmets and flak jackets

49. Bridgestone

50. Callaway

3

IT ALL BEGINS AT MECCA

THE MASTERS

1. What was the original name of the Masters?

2. True-False. An amateur has never won the Masters.

3. Who is the youngest player ever to win the Masters?
   a. Jack Nicklaus
   b. Henry Picard
   c. Seve Ballesteros
   d. Arnold Palmer

4. Who were the architects of Augusta National?

5. True-False. Bobby Jones never played in the Masters, the tournament he created.

Wayne hits his ball out-of-bounds onto a hard surface road. The ball bounces for about 100 yards, strikes a car and bounces back onto the course and in-bounds. Can Wayne play this ball?

Yes. Since Wayne's ball has come to rest in-bounds, it is indeed in-bounds despite its journey.

---

6. Who was tournament director of the Masters for 40 years?

7. Name the player who made a double eagle on the 69th (par 5, 15th hole) to catch the leader in a Masters?
   a. Craig Wood
   b. Gene Sarazen
   c. Greg Norman
   d. Arnold Palmer

8. What two-time Master's champion missed the cut both years that he defended his championship?

9. What tradition does an amateur player in The Masters take part in when he tees it up at Augusta National?

10. How many Masters Championships has Jack Nicklaus won?
    a. 4
    b. 5
    c. 6
    d. 7

11. What holes at Augusta National make up "Amen Corner"?

12. Only two players have won back-to-back Masters Championships. Name them.

13. Who holds the record for the highest winning score in Masters' history?
    a. Sam Snead and Jack Burke Jr.
    b. Ben Hogan
    c. Horton Smith
    d. Ben Crenshaw and Tom Watson

14. Name the infamous par three hole at Augusta National that is protected in front by Rae's Creek.

15. Who is the oldest player to win the Masters?
    a. Jack Nicklaus
    b. Gary Player
    c. Ray Floyd
    d. Ben Crenshaw

16. Of the following golf greats, who has never won a Masters?
    a. Billy Casper
    b. Lee Trevino
    c. Ben Hogan
    d. Byron Nelson

17. The lowest winning score for the masters is held by two players. Name them.

18. True-False. A Masters Champion automatically is invited to play in the tournament for life.

19. Describe the logo for the Augusta National course.

20. What is the name of the road leading into Augusta National?

21. What two companies have been television sponsors for every Masters?

22. What is the name of the building where the Masters Champion is presented with the traditional green jacket?

23. Of the top 25 money winners of the 1991 PGA Tour, how many of them have won the Masters? Name them.

24. Who has played in the most Masters tournaments?

25. Name the amateur who had a four-stroke lead on the final day only to shoot an 80 and lose by one stroke.
    a. Billy Joe Patton
    b. Bobby Jones
    c. Jack Nicklaus
    d. Ken Venturi

26. Name the amateur who was in the lead at the Masters with just five holes to go and drove his ball into the water.

Harold's ball is not in a hazard but he wants to chip the ball through a sand trap and onto the green. Before playing the shot, he walks up to the trap and takes a swing to test the consistency of the sand. He then plays a shot that skims through the sand and lands next to the pin. His opponent yells foul.

Since Harold's ball is not in a hazard, the rules involving a hazard do not apply. There is no penalty.

So You Think You Know Golf?

27. In 1968, this player had the winning score but was disqualified for signing an incorrect scorecard. Name him.

28. In 1960, this player had to make birdies on 17 and 18 to win the Masters. He did it!
    a. Gary Player
    b. Arnold Palmer
    c. Cary Middlecoff
    d. Jack Nicklaus

Brian's ball lies against a tree trunk. In order to punch the ball out to the fairway, he bends the shaft of his putter to accommodate the tree trunk. He successfully hits the ball out of trouble. Is this legal?

Brian must be disqualified for changing the playing characteristics of a club and then playing a shot with it. Rule 4-2 requires disqualification as the penalty.

29. What year did the Masters begin?
    a. 1905
    b. 1927
    c. 1934
    d. 1939

30. True-False. Since its beginning, the Masters has been played every year.

31. Who holds the record for the lowest single round in Masters play?

John and Tim are playing a match in the club championship. After holing out a ten-foot putt on the 17th hole to win the match (2 and 1), John accepts Tim's congratulations. When they get to the bar, John discovers that he played a wrong ball for his second shot to the green on 17. John and Tim ask you to make a ruling.

Rule 2-5 states that any claim must be made before reaching the next tee or, in this case, before the players leave the putting green. The only exception would be if John had intentionally and knowingly played a wrong ball. The penalty would be loss of match.

32. Name the player who had his invitation to the Masters withdrawn because of newspaper stories linking him to underworld figures.

33. Name the player who made a record six consecutive birdies in the 1975 Masters.

34. Who was the only player in Masters history to lead in all four rounds?
    a. Jack Nicklaus
    b. Ray Floyd
    c. Gary Player
    d. Johnny Miller

35. Who won the first Masters ever played?

So You Think You Know Golf?

36. Jack Nicklaus has the most Masters Championships. Only one player has won four. Name him.
    a. Ben Hogan
    b. Sam Snead
    c. Gene Sarazen
    d. Arnold Palmer

37. True-False. Jack Nicklaus holds the record for winning a Masters by the most strokes—nine.

38. True-False. Members of Augusta National and former champions may not wear their green jackets outside of the course.

39. True-False. The defending champion of the Masters must host an opening night dinner for all the former champions.

40. In 1979, Larry Nelson made his first appearance at the Masters. What was so significant about it?

IT ALL BEGINS AT MECCA

THE MASTERS

1. The Augusta National Invitational Tournament

2. True

3. c. Seve Ballesteros was 23 years old when he won in 1980.

4. Alister Mackenzie and Bobby Jones.

5. False. He played in the first 12.

6. Clifford Roberts

7. b. Gene Sarazen

8. Seve Ballersteros

9. He is paired with a former Masters Champion.

10. c. 6

11. the 11th, 12th and 13th

12. Jack Nicklaus (1965-1966) and Nick Faldo (1989-1990)

13. a. Sam Snead (1954) and Jack Burke Jr. (1956) with a score of 289.

14. the 12th hole

15. Jack Nicklaus—46 years old in 1986

16. b. Lee Trevino

17. Jack Nicklaus and Ray Floyd (271)

18. True

19. The Augusta National Logo is an outline of the United States with a flagstick placed on Augusta, Georgia.

20. Magnolia Lane

21. Travelers Insurance and Cadillac

22. Butler Cabin

23. One—Craig Stadler

24. Sam Snead—44

25. d. Ken Venturi

26. Billy Joe Patton

27. Roberto De Vicenzo

28. b. Arnold Palmer

29. c. 1934

30. False. No tournaments were held 1943-1945 (World War II)

31. Nick Price—63 in 1986

32. Jumbo Ozaki—he was later re-invited.

33. Johnny Miller

34. Ray Floyd

35. Horton Smith

36. d. Arnold Palmer

37. True

38. True

39. True

40. He forgot his clubs.

4

"CARRY YOUR BAG, SIR?"

THE CADDIES

1. About how much are caddies paid on the PGA Tour?

2. Who is the only caddy to appear on a U.S. Postage Stamp? Why is that stamp prized by collectors?

3. Who was William Gunn in caddy lore?

4. What top player on the LPGA usually has her husband caddy for her?

5. What caddy on the 1986 PGA Tour went on to win a PGA Tour tournament himself that year?

6. What Touring pro has his sister caddy for him?

So You Think You Know Golf?

In a medal tournament, Mike hits a long drive straight down the middle of the fairway. He is playing a Maxfli HT #3 ball. When he comes to the spot in the fairway to play his shot, he discovers two Maxfli HT #3's lying next to each other. Neither ball has any distinguishing marks, so he chooses one and hits it onto the green. After the round, he mentions the incident to you. Ruling, please.

Mike has to be disqualified for playing the "wrong ball." He was not able to properly identify his ball. (It's always a good idea to place your mark on a ball.)

7. In the 1986 British Open, a player found out that his caddie was awaiting trial for murder. Who was this frightened star?

8. What PGA Tour player had the habit of having his caddie kneel behind the ball to help him line his putt while he putted? (His use of this technique forced a rule change to prohibit it.)

9. Why do caddies pick the ball out of the hole for the players?

10. On the Tour, which caddy tends the pin first and which caddy replaces it at the end?

11. Who was considered "The Grand Old Man of Tour Caddies"?

12. Name the three leading caddy scholarship funds in America.

13. In the 1986 Anhauser-Busch Classic, this pro was disqualified because he ran out of balls after his caddy had discarded them to lighten his load.

    a. Steve Pate
    b. Bill Kratzert
    c. Hal Sutton
    d. Billy Mayfair

So You Think You Know Golf?

14. What is the name of the tournament in which Tour caddies play for up to $10,000 in prize money?

15. What was the last PGA Tournament to require that only local caddies be used?

    a. 1990 Honda Classic
    b. 1988 Tournament of Champions
    c. 1985 Western Open
    d. 1987 Phoenix Open

16. What is a "caddy swing"?

17. Translate the following caddy slang.

    "Being on someone"
    "A good bag"
    "Warming the eggs"
    "Clubbing your man"
    "A safari"

18. What Tour pro tosses his putter to his caddy in such a manner that he is called "Flipper"?

19. If a caddy is carrying two bags and is struck by a ball, who is considered to be his player according to the Rules of Golf?

20. Where does the word "caddy" come from?

While playing in a match for the club championship, Linda hits her ball into heavy rough. While searching for the ball, her caddie accidentally kicks the ball out of the rough and onto the fairway. Ruling, please.

Linda must replace her ball to its original lie. There is no penalty (Rule 18-3a).

Wally is a professional golfer. On December 31st, he declares that he is an amateur and quits his job as a club professional. Two weeks later, he enters a tournament for amateurs and wins it. Some of the other competitors cry foul. Was Wally free to play as an amateur?

Wally is disqualified. Under the Rules of Amateur Status, he had to have applied for reinstatement as an amateur and serve a prescribed waiting period.

21. Match these caddies with their long-time association to these famous players.

CADDIES	PLAYERS
Pete Bender	Tom Watson
Willie Cemetery Poteet	Lee Trevino
Rabbit Dyer	Arnold Palmer
Angelo Argea	Gary Player
Iron Man Avery	Greg Norman
Herman Mitchell	Jack Nicklaus
Bruce Edwards	Ike Eisenhower

22. What is the "caddy rule"?

23. In the early days of golf, caddies were classified as _____.

    a. servants
    b. professionals
    c. valets
    d. partners

24. True-False. A player may change caddies during a tournament round.

25. In the 1890s, what piece of equipment was added that greatly helped caddies?

26. True-False. Caddies on the PGA Tour are paid to wear hats and visors to promote certain products.

27. True-False. On the Senior Tour, where players are allowed to ride carts, a caddy may not ride in the cart with his player.

28. What LPGA Pro caddied on the men's Tour to gain knowledge?

29. True-False. In Japan, at many exclusive clubs, most caddies are women.

30. Who caddied for Jack Nicklaus when he won the 1986 Masters?

31. Upon arriving at the ball, a Tour caddie will often say, "157 and 8." What do these figures mean?

"CARRY YOUR BAG, SIR?"

THE CADDIES

1. Caddies on the PGA Tour are paid about $300 per week plus 5% of their player's earnings.

2. Eddie Lowery appeared with Francis Ouimet on the 1988 stamp issued to commemorate Ouimet's 1913 U.S. Open victory at The Country Club in Brookline, Massachusetts. The stamp is of particular interest to collectors because it is a very rare instance for someone who is depicted on a stamp to still be alive.

3. William Gunn was a caddie at the Royal Edinburgh Golfing Society. Known as "Caddie Willie" or "Daft Willie," he was the subject of early golf art showing him in ragged clothes but with a brilliant red coat.

4. Juli Inkster has her husband, Brian, caddy for her.

5. Mark Calcavecchia caddied for Ken Green in the early part of 1986. He later won the Southwest Classic that same year.

6. Ken Green

7. Gary Player

8. Johnny Miller had his caddy kneel to help his alignment. The Rules of Golf were changed to outlaw this practice in 1986.

9. Most caddies wear sneakers. If the players continually walked near the hole with their spikes the area around the hole would become rough with spike marks. As a courtesy to their fellow players they have their caddies pick the ball out of the hole when possible.

10. The caddy whose player is putting first will tend the pin first. The caddy whose player putts last must replace it.

11. The late Lee Lynch caddied on the Tour well into his 70s.

12. The three national caddy scholarship funds are: the Chick Evans, the Francis Ouimet and the Jack Burke.

13. Bill Kratzert

14. The Caddy Classic

15. In 1985 the Western Open became the last tournament to require local caddies on a PGA Tour event.

16. A "caddy swing" is considered to be a smooth, compact swing developed from repeated practice while waiting for a bag or player.

17. "Being on someone"—to have a player assigned in a tournament.

    "A good bag"—to caddy for someone who has a chance to win the tournament or is a good tipper.

    "Warming the eggs"—the practice of carrying golf balls in a pant pocket in order to warm them on a cold day.

    "Clubbing your man"—advising the player on the correct club to use for a shot.

    "A safari"—to caddy for a player who has had an awful round.

18. Ken Green

19. The player who hit the shot is considered to be the player's caddy for rules purposes.

20. Mary Queen of Scots called her young attendants in her court "cadets." The French pronunciation of *cadet* is "Cad-day." Thus, when Mary played golf her attendants became known as caddies.

21. Pete Bender—Greg Norman
    Willie Poteet—Ike Eisenhower
    Rabbit Dyer—Gary Player
    Angelo Argea—Jack Nicklaus
    Iron Man Avery—Arnold Palmer
    Herman Mitchell—Lee Trevino
    Bruce Edwards—Tom Watson

22. Rule 6-4 is known as the "Caddy Rule." It states, "For any breach of a Rule by his caddy, the player incurs the applicable penalty."

23. Caddies were once categorized as professionals. It was not until the 1950s that the USGA removed the professional status from caddies who were over the age of 18.

24. True

25. Golf Bags—up until this time, caddies often had to carry the clubs in loose fashion.

26. True

27. True. The 1984 rule was intended to help the gallery keep pace with the players who may ride in a cart.

28. Michelle McGann caddied for Dave Stocton in 1987.

29. True

30. Jack Nicklaus II

31. yards to the front of the green and then yards to the pin

5

BELOVED BATTLEFIELDS

THE COURSES

1. Besides Mother Nature, who was the genius behind the design of Pebble Beach?

2. The British Open has only been played once outside of England and Scotland. Name the course.

3. What famous British Open Course has hazards named, "Jackie's Burn" and "Barry Burn"?
   - a. Turnberry
   - b. St. Andrews
   - c. Carnoustie
   - d. County Down

4. Who designed the famous Pinehurst Number 2 course?

5. What famous course and site of U.S. Opens features wicker baskets instead of flags on its flagsticks?

6. Since 1978, the LPGA Championship has been held on the same course. Name it.

Anthony is very particular about his equipment. Before each round, he places a light coat of oil on the clubface of each iron to keep them shiny. Is this OK according to the Rules?

Anthony may indeed be violating the Rules of Golf in regard to applying a foreign substance that may influence the flight of the ball.

7. What course was the site of the first U.S. Open and the first U.S. Amateur?

    a. The Country Club
    b. St. Andrews (New York)
    c. Chicago Golf Club
    d. Newport Country Club

8. Which famous championship course began as a gift from an employer to his workers?

9. Name the two touring pros who founded the Champions course in Texas.

10. What course is famous for its "church pew" bunkers?

11. Where did the great course in New Jersey called Baltusrol get its name from?

12. What course is said to be built "on the most expensive piece of real estate in the world"?

13. On the 17th hole at The Country Club, there is an infamous bunker just at the turn of the dogleg. What is its name and why is it so called?

At the end of her round in a medal tournament Kathy signs her scorecard with a score of 76. A few minutes later she discovers that she misread a 4 for a 6 on one hole and that her real score is 74. A 74 would win the tournament for her. Ruling please.

Barbara must keep her 76 as per Rule 6-6d.

14. Name the course that is the site of the Heritage Classic on the PGA Tour.

    a. Heritage
    b. The National
    c. Harbour Town
    d. Williamsburg

15. What do the "white faces" of Merion refer to?

16. Name the course that hosted a U.S. Women's Open whose logo is a witch.

17. What is an executive course?

18. What is a Cayman Course?

19. Why do many courses in Japan have two greens?

20. What is the longest golf course in the World?

21. What was the first golf course in the United States?

22. Which of the following great courses is open to the public?

    a. Pebble Beach
    b. Pine Valley
    c. Scioto
    d. The Country Club

23. What course hosts the Tournament of Champions at the start of each year?

24. What course has Lee Trevino said does not "fit" his game?

25. What is Arnold Palmer's home course?

26. What PGA Tour Course features consecutive par threes and par fives?

Willie's ball is completely plugged in a sand trap and covered with sand. In order to identify his ball, Willie begins to brush off some sand. In doing so, the ball suddenly becomes dislodged, rolls out of its hole and comes to rest in the middle of the trap in a good lie. Ruling, please?

Replace the ball to its original lie. There is no penalty.

27. What course is annually rated number one in *Golf Digest* for "tradition"?
    a. Shimmecock Hills
    b. The Country Club
    c. Augusta National
    d. Pine Valley

28. What course was selected as the site for the Ryder Cup before it was finished being built?

29. Where is Mid Ocean, the famous resort course located?
    a. Midway Island
    b. Puerto Rico
    c. Bermuda
    d. Hawaii

30. Where is the famous Oak Hill course, located?
    a. Illinois
    b. New York
    c. Michigan
    d. New Jersey

31. Name the architect who designed two courses—one, the site of a U.S. Open, and the other the site of a U.S. Women's Open. Bonus points for naming the courses.

32. How many golf courses are there in Italy?

    a. 0
    b. 5
    c. 25
    d. 80

Bill's ball is lodged in a tree about ten feet off of the ground. He stands on his golf cart and successfully plays the ball out of the tree. Is this legal?

Bill is "building a stance" under the Rules of Golf. This is a two-stroke penalty or loss of hole.

---

33. On which course did Jack Nicklaus win the British Open twice?

    a. Troon
    b. St. Andrews
    c. Carnoustie
    d. Turnberry

34. For what material of golf courses is Pete Dye famous?

35. Name the five founding courses of the USGA.

36. Which state has built the most courses in the past ten years?

    a. California
    b. South Carolina
    c. Florida
    d. Texas

37. At what course is "Beman's Road" located?

38. Name the golf resort that was first to offer 72 holes.

39. What golf club is the longest in continuous existence in the world?

40. What was the site of the British Open's 100th anniversary?
    a. St. Andrews
    b. Royal Birkdale
    c. Royal St. Georges
    d. Royal Lytham

41. True-False. Pinehurst has never hosted a U.S. Open.

42. Where did Arnold Palmer win his U.S. Amateur title?
    a. LaTrobe C.C.
    b. Pebble Beach
    c. Scioto
    d. Country Club of Detroit

43. This course has hosted three U.S. Opens—all ending in playoffs. Name this great course.

After Art flubs his ball in a sand trap, it remains in the same trap. He uses his sand wedge to smooth the trap where he has just made a stroke then hits his next shot onto the green. His opponent claims that he has illegally grounded his club between shots. You are asked to make a ruling.

There is no penalty. Art was not attempting to test the sand.

44. On which course was the first British Open held in 1860?

    a. St. Andrews

    b. Prestwick

    c. Troon

    d. Royal Birkdale

45. This British Open Course was turned into an airfield for both World Wars. Name it.

46. On which famous course is the 18th hole protected by the "valley of sin"?

47. This long flat course was the site of the 1958 U.S. Open where the best score (Tommy Bolt, 283) was three over par. Name it.

    a. Oak Tree

    b. Quail Creek

    c. Southern Hills

    d. Tulsa C.C.

48. In 1926 Bobby Jones knocked a long iron 175 yards from a deep bunker to enable him to win his first British Open. A plaque lies on the spot from where he made the great shot. Name the course.

49. In 1940 this famous course produced the U.S. Amateur and U.S. Open champions. Name the course.

50. What city hosts the World Amateur Championship for handicappers of all levels?

51. What is the oldest course in North America?

52. What is the width of a hole?

53. What famous course has a sand trap so large it is called "Hell's half acre"?

54. Two of the holes at St. Andrews are named after golfers. Name the men so honored.

Walter and Jerry are playing a match. Walter hits a great five-iron shot directly at the pin. The ball strikes the flag and becomes entangled in it. Jerry claims that Walter must take a drop as this is a case of an unplayable lie. Ruling, please?

Walter may drop his ball next to the hole. There is no penalty according to USGA's decisions.

55. Match the course to its architect.

Oakmont	Pete Dye and Jack Nicklaus
Baltusrol	Henry C. Fownes
The Country Club	Robert Trent Jones
Harbour Town	A.W. Tillinghast
Merion	Hugh Wilson
Firestone (South)	Geoffrey Cornish

56. True-False. A hole cannot be placed closer than three feet from the edge of the green.

57. What famous course did Jack Nicklaus grow up on? Bonus points for naming who designed it.

58. Walter Hagen was named the first head pro at this course.

   a. Oakmont

   b. Merion

   c. Seminole

   d. Oakland Hills

59. What course is consistently rated the most difficult in America by *Golf Digest*?

    a. Pine Valley
    b. Augusta National
    c. Baltusrol
    d. Medinah

60. What course on the PGA Tour is called "The Blue Monster"?

61. What four courses are traditionally used for the Bob Hope Desert Classic?

BELOVED BATTLEFIELDS

THE COURSES

1. Jack Neville

2. Royal Portrush in Northern Ireland

3. c. Carnoustie

4. Donald Ross

5. Merion

6. Jack Nicklaus Golf Center, King's Island, Ohio

7. d. Newport Country Club

8. Firestone

9. Jimmy Demaret and Jack Burke

10. Oakmont

11. The original land belonged to a farmer named Baltus Roll.

12. Cypress Point

13. Harry Vardon landed in what's called the Vardon Bunker in his battle with young Francis Ouimet during the 1913 U.S. Open.

14. c. Harbour Town

15. its sand traps

16. Salem Country Club, Peabody, Massachusetts

17. An executive course is a course that has shortened holes and is generally easier and faster to play (thus the name for busy executives) than a regulation course.

18. A cayman course is an extremely short course that is played with a ball that has a very low compression and thus would not travel far.

19. The Japanese climate has wide extremes. To keep grass suitable for putting, they will have one green of bent grass for warmer months and a tougher strength of grass from Korea called korai that holds up well in the colder weather.

20. The world's longest course, according to *The Guinness Book of World Records,* is the par 77, 8,325 yard International Golf Course in Bolton, Massachusetts.

21. St. Andrews in Yonkers, New York

22. a. Pebble Beach

23. La Costa, Carlsbad, California

24. Augusta National, home of the Masters

25. LaTrobe C.C., in Pennsylvania

26. Cypress Point

27. Augusta National

28. Kiawah in 1991

29. c. Bermuda

30. b. New York

31. William Flynn the Cascades (Virginia) and Cherry Hills (Colorado)

32. d. 80

33. b. St. Andrews

34. railroad ties

35. St. Andrews (New York)
    Newport Country Club
    The Country Club
    Shinnecock Hills
    Chicago Country Club

36. c. Florida

37. Merion—in the 1966 U.S. Amateur, Deane Beman drove out of bounds on the 15th hole and onto the infamous road to lose the tournament.

38. Pinehurst

39. Honorable Company of Edinburgh Golfers at Muirfield

40. b. Royal Birkdale

So You Think You Know Golf?

41. True

42. d. Country Club of Detroit

43. The Country Club

44. b. Prestwick

45. Turnberry

46. St. Andrews

47. c. Southern Hills

48. Royal Lytham

49. Winged Foot in New York—member Dick Chapman won the Amateur and head pro Craig Wood won the Open.

50. Myrtle Beach, South Carolina

51. Royal Montreal (1873)

52. 4.25 inches

53. Pine Valley

54. Bobby Jones (10th) and Tom Morris (18th)

55. Oakmont—Henry C. Fownes
Baltusrol—A.W. Tillinghast
The Country Club—Geoffrey Cornish
Harbour Town—Pete Dye and Jack Nicklaus
Merion—Hugh Wilson
Firestone (South)—Robert Trent Jones

56. False. The Rules of Golf do not make any specifications in this regard.

57. Scioto in Columbus, Ohio—Donald Ross, architect

58. d. Oakland Hills in 1918

59. d. Medinah is consistently rated as the toughest.

60. The Doral Country Club in Miami, Florida

61. TPC at PGA West, Bermuda Dunes, Indian Wells and Tamarisk are the frequent sites used by the Bob Hope Desert Classic.

6

FOR THE LOVE OF IT

THE AMATEURS

1. What U.S. and British Open champion used up to 26 clubs to win, prompting the 14 club limit rule?

2. How old was Bobby Jones when he played in his first U.S. Amateur?
    a. 14
    b. 19
    c. 27
    d. 30

3. Name the amateur who finished second in the Masters for two consecutive years?
    a. Jay Sigel
    b. Ken Venturi
    c. Charles Coe
    d. Bobby Jones

4. Which of the players below never won a U.S. Amateur Championship?
    a. Arnold Palmer
    b. Tom Watson
    c. Lanny Wadkins
    d. Jack Nicklaus

5. Name the only player to win the U.S. Amateur five times.

6. Who was the last amateur to win the U.S. Open?
    a. Bobby Jones
    b. Francis Ouimet
    c. Lawson Little
    d. Johnny Goodman

7. In 1989, The European team won the Walker Cup over the United States. What year was their last prior win?

8. In 1988, this woman won both the U.S. Women's Amateur and U.S. Publinks championships?
    a. Kay Cockerill
    b. Pearl Sinn
    c. Vicki Goetze
    d. Deb Richard

9. Which of these great players has never won the Women's U.S. Amateur?

    a. Pat Bradley
    b. Juli Imkster
    c. Joanne Carner
    d. Beth Daniel

10. Who was the only man ever to be ranked number one amateur by *Golf Digest* for three consecutive years?

    a. Scott Verplank
    b. Jay Sigel
    c. Jack Nicklaus
    d. Ben Crenshaw

Bob and Tony are playing a match in their club championship. Since their region has been having a severe drought, the fairways are dry and hard. They mutually agree to take preferred lies in the fairway for their match only. Another competitor complains. Is this legal?

By agreeing to waive the Rules, both players can be disqualified under Rule 1-3.

---

11. From 1975 to 1988, only one man was ranked in *Golf Digest's* top ten amateurs. Name him.

12. Of the players on the 1992 PGA Senior Tour, only three have won U.S. Amateur titles. Name all three.

13. Who was the last amateur to win the British Open?
   a. Deane Beman
   b. Lawson Little
   c. Charles Coe
   d. Bobby Jones

14. What was Bobby Jones' occupation?

15. Who was the only player to be named first team All-American for each of his four years in college as of 1992?
   a. Gary Hallberg
   b. Arnold Palmer
   c. Jack Nicklaus
   d. Jerry Pate

16. Name two amateurs who have won PGA Tour events since 1980.

17. Under the Rules of Golf, what is the amount of retail value of a prize that an amateur may receive?
   a. $400
   b. $500
   c. $700
   d. $1,000

18. Which college has produced the most individual NCAA champions?
   a. Wake Forest
   b. Houston
   c. Florida State
   d. Yale

19. In 1972, two players from Texas tied to win NCAA individual champion and are now famous on the PGA Tour. Name them.

20. Name the only two golfers who have received the Sullivan Award, as the outstanding AAU Amateur Athlete of the Year.

21. In 1955, the USGA instituted the Bob Jones Award for distinguished sportsmanship. Who was the first recipient?

22. Name the coach who has won 16 NCAA golf championships.

23. What is the name of the trophy given to the winner of the U.S. Amateur Open?

24. What handicap must an amateur have in order to be allowed to attempt to qualify for the U.S. Amateur?

25. How many amateurs have won the Masters?

26. Name the amateur who made a hole-in-one and finished second in the 1954 Masters.

Harvey is playing in a medal tournament. He is having a bad day putting and sends his caddy to the locker room to get his other putter. He discards his original putter and plays the last three holes with the putter from the locker room. Is this legal?

Since Harvey's putter was not deemed unfit for play because of normal damage, he may not change clubs. He is given a four-stroke penalty, two strokes per hole but not to exceed four strokes in total.

27. What year did Bobby Jones win his "grand slam"?

28. Following his college career at Wake Forest, what career move did Arnold Palmer make?

29. What U.S. Amateur champion broke the world pole vault record three years later?

30. Who was the youngest man ever to win a U.S. Amateur title?

    a. Bobby Jones
    b. Jay Sigel
    c. Robert Gardner
    d. Phil Mickelson

31. Who is the oldest winner of the U.S. Amateur?

32. Who has played in the most Walker Cup matches?

    a. Ben Crenshaw
    b. Ted Bishop
    c. Joe Carr
    d. Jay Sigel

Margaret's ball flies into a sand trap and lands next to a dead squirrel. She asks if she may remove the squirrel. What is your answer?

Sorry, the squirrel is a loose impediment and cannot be removed from a hazard.

---

33. Who won the U.S. Women's Amateur six times?

    a. Babe Zaharias
    b. Betsy Rawls
    c. Glenna Vare
    d. JoAnne Gunderson (Carner)

34. What are the names of the team matches between the best women amateurs of the United States and Great Britain?

35. Who is the only amateur to win the U.S. Women's Open?
    a. Kay Cockerill
    b. Catherine LaCoste
    c. Babe Zaharias
    d. Mickey Wright

36. Who holds the all time record for most matches won in the U.S. Amateur?
    a. Jay Sigel
    b. Bobby Jones
    c. Bill Campbell
    d. Charles Evans

37. Who was the last woman to win back to back Amateur titles?
    a. Pearle Sinn
    b. Beth Daniel
    c. Kay Cockerill
    d. Fay Crocker

38. True-False. The British have won more Walker Cups than the United States.

Touring pro, Mike, hits a drive that lands in the gallery. Upon reaching the spot where the ball lies, he finds it in a pile of ice from a spectator's soft drink. Mike claims that ice is a form of casual water and that he is entitled to relief without penalty. You are called to make a ruling.

While ice is considered casual water, ice from an artificial source is not. Mike has to play it as it lies.

39. Name the player who never lost a Walker Cup match in eight meetings.

40. What PGA Tour player won back to back U.S. Amateur Public Links Championships in 1980-1981?

41. True-False. The Walker Cup was donated by President George Walker Bush's grandfather.

FOR THE LOVE OF IT

THE AMATEURS

1. Lawson Little was famous for his trunk of clubs.

2. a. 14

3. c. Charles Coe

4. b. Tom Watson

5. Bobby Jones won in 1924, 1925, 1927, 1928 and 1930.

6. d. Johnny Goodman was the last amateur to win the U.S. Open (1933).

7. 1971

8. b. Pearl Sinn

9. a. Pat Bradley

10. c. Jack Nicklaus was the top ranked amateur from 1959 to 1961.

11. Jay Sigel

12. Gene Littler, Arnold Palmer and Jack Nicklaus

13. d. Bobby Jones was the last amateur to win the British Open (1930).

14. He was a lawyer.

15. a. Gary Hallberg

16. Scott Verplank won the 1985 Western Open and Phil Mickelson won the 1991 Northern Telecom Open.

17. b. $500

18. d. Yale (13 champions)

19. Ben Crenshaw and Tom Kite

20. Bobby Jones and Lawson Little

21. Francis Ouimet

22. Dave Williams at the University of Houston

23. The Havermeyer Trophy

24. A player must have a handicap of two or less.

25. To date, no amateur has won the Masters.

26. Billy Joe Patton

27. In 1930, Bobby Jones won the U.S. Open, the British Open and the British and U.S. Amateurs.

28. He joined the Coast Guard.

29. Robert Gardner

30. c. Robert Gardner (at age 19)

31. Jack Westland, at age 47

32. Joe Carr, Great Britain, 10

33. c. Glenna Vare

34. The Curtis Cup

35. b. Catherine LaCoste

36. d. Charles Evans

37. c. Kay Cockerill (1986-1987)

38. False

39. William Campbell

40. Jodie Mudd

41. True

So You Think You Know Golf?

7
WORDS AND PICTURES

1. Name the two famous pros who hosted the long running television golf show, "Shell's Wonderful World of Golf."

2. What is the title of Ben Hogan's autobiography?

3. Who wrote, *The Green Road Home*, after spending a year as a caddy on the PGA Tour?
   a. George Plympton
   b. Herman Mitchell
   c. Michael Bamberger
   d. Dan Jenkins

4. Name the three stars of the golf movie, *Caddy Shack*.

5. Who wrote the book, *Dead Solid Perfect*, which went on to become a movie?

6. What is the name of Jack Nicklaus' best-selling book/video instruction package?

7. Who is the executive editor of *Golf Digest*?

8. What is the name of Arnold Palmer's autobiography?

9. What is the name of the video made from old 16mm instructional films of Bobby Jones?

Bill has placed a mark on top of his irons to help him align the club and ball on the sweet spot or center. Another player complains. Is this legal?

This is illegal. Any devices to assist alignment on clubs other than putters is prohibited.

---

10. Who wrote, *Pigeons, Marks, Hustlers and Other Golf Bettors You Can Beat?*

    a. Tommy Bolt
    b. Lee Trevino
    c. Jimmy the Greek
    d. Sam Snead

11. Name the three books that Bobby Jones wrote on golf.

12. Seve Ballesteros' instruction book, *Natura Golf*, was co-authored by what famous senior editor of *Golf Magazine*?

13. *Golf Digest* apologized for an article that offended Boston's Irish community just prior to the 1988 U.S. Open at The Country Club. Who wrote the article?

14. What was the first golf tournament ever to be televised?

15. What is the subtitle of *The Rules Of Golf*?

16. Golf announcer Jay Randolph is now involved in another occupation as well. Name it.

17. Match the videos with their pros.

Golf Like a Pro	Arnold Palmer
Golf From the Other Side	Ben Crenshaw
The Art of Putting	Jimmy Ballard
The Golf Connection	Bob Charles
Practice Like a Pro	Billy Casper

18. What Pulitzer prize winning cartoonist appears in *Golf Digest*?

Playing in a match, Steve shanks his shot badly. The ball strikes his opponent's caddy on the leg. Ruling, please.

Steve may replay the shot with no penalty (Rule 19-2b).

While on the putting green, Kathy asks her caddie to move his foot a little so that she can use it as an aiming point for her putt. Is this legal?

This is a violation of Rule 8-2. It means a two-stroke penalty or loss of hole in match play.

19. What ABC broadcaster was Senior Executive Director of the USGA?

20. What CBS broadcaster was chastised by the Masters tournament committee for referring to the gallery as a "mob"?

21. What subject does the Masters prohibit television announcers from speaking about on air?
    a. course conditions
    b. prize money
    c. Clifford Roberts
    d. size of the gallery

22. What famous sportswriter urged Babe Didrickson to take up golf?
    a. Herbert Warren Wind
    b. Alistair Cooke
    c. Grantland Rice
    d. Charles Price

23. Which of these TV golf announcers won a U.S. Amateur Championship?
    a. Jay Randolph
    b. Ben Wright
    c. Steve Melnyk
    d. Gary McCord

24. What tournament changed its format from match to medal to accommodate television?

25. Who wrote the classic, *A Golf Story*?

26. What tournament traditionally attracts the largest television audience?
    a. U. S. Open
    b. British Open
    c. The Masters
    d. PGA Championship

27. What sportswriter coined the term "Amen Corner" about the three difficult holes at Augusta National's back nine?

28. Who wrote the classic, *The Glorious World of Golf*?

29. What CBS announcer has won a U.S. Open?

30. What educational director of the PGA wrote, *The New Golf Mind*?

31. *The Game of Golf and the Printed Word* sold for $100. Who wrote it?

32. What former Tour pro turned orthopedic surgeon and now writes a health column for *Golf Digest*?

33. What is the name of Doug Sander's book on golf hustling?

34. What golf announcer said, "There are two things that these guys on tour do not like: playing in the wind and me dating their sisters."?

So You Think You Know Golf?

35. Who wrote the classic, *The Golf Courses of the British Isles* in 1911?

36. What is the name of the award given annually by the Golf Writers' Association of America for outstanding contributions to golf?

37. Who wrote the famous instructional book, *Five Lessons: The Modern Fundamentals of Golf*?

38. Who wrote *The Why Book of Golf*? (Bonus point for a correct answer.)

39. Who wrote the comprehensive history of golf book entitled, *Golf, Its History, People and Events*?

40. What was the name of Harry Vardon's famous book published in 1905?

41. Who sang the hit golf song, "It Went Straight Down the Middle" (his son became a U.S. Open champion).

42. In 1990, what trading card company came out with 100 PGA Tour cards in its Inaugural set?
    a. Topps
    b. Fleer
    c. Upper Deck
    d. Pro Set

On the tee, John uses his heel to dig up a little mound of turf. He then places the ball on top of the mound and plays a tee shot. Is this legal?

This is legal on the tee.

WORDS AND PICTURES

1. Gene Sarazen and Jimmy Demaret

2. *Follow the Sun*

3. c. Michael Bamberger

4. Chevy Chase, Rodney Dangerfield and Bill Murray

5. Dan Jenkins

6. *Golf My Way*

7. Jerry Tarde

8. *Go for Broke*

9. *How I Play Golf*

10. d. Sam Snead

11. *Down the Fairway*
    Bobby Jones on Golf
    Golf is My Game

12. John Andrisani

13. Peter Dobereiner

14. The Tam O'Shanter World Championship, August 23, 1953

15. And the Rules of Amateur Status

16. He's a golf course architect.

17. *Golf Like a Pro*—Billy Casper
    Golf from the Other Side—Bob Charles
    The Art of Putting—Ben Crenshaw
    The Golf Connection—Jimmy Ballard
    Practice Like a Pro—Arnold Palmer

18. Paul Szep

19. Frank Hannigan

20. Jack Whitaker

21. b. prize money

22. c. Grantland Rice

23. c. Steve Melnyk

24. The PGA Championship

25. Charles Price

26. c. The Masters

27. Herbert Warren Wind

28. Peter Dobereiner

29. Ken Venturi

30. Dr. Gary Wiren

31. Richard Donavan and Joseph Murdoch

32. Dr. Bill Mallon

33. *Action on the First Tee*

34. Gary McCord

35. Bernard Darwin

36. The Richardson Award

37. Ben Hogan

38. Bill Kroen

39. Will Grimsley

40. *The Complete Golfer*

41. Bing Crosby—Nathaniel Crosby, his son, won the U.S. Amateur in 1981.

42. d. Pro Set

8

FOLLOWING THE SUN

THE
PROFESSIONALS

1. Name the only man to win a U.S. Open, Masters and a British Open in the 1980s.

2. Who is the only player to be the PGA Tour's leading money winner for four consecutive years?

3. Who was the first man on the PGA Tour to earn more than $200,000 in one year?
   a. Arnold Palmer
   b. Ben Hogan
   c. Billy Casper
   d. Sam Snead

4. Who was the first pro to break one million dollars in career earnings?

Jeff and Doug are playing in a medal tournament. Doug is putting first. He removes the flagstick and places it about ten feet behind the hole. His putt is struck too hard and heads for the flagstick. Before it strikes the flagstick, Jeff runs over and picks it up as the ball passes by without striking it. Is this legal?

So much for being a good Samaritan. Jeff gets a two-stroke penalty since he influenced the position or movement of a ball.

---

5. For what is the Vardon Trophy given on the PGA Tour?

6. Sam Snead has won 84 PGA tournaments. Who has finished second the most times?

7. What pro's trademark for his equipment and clothing is an umbrella?

8. What do the following Tour players all have in common?

> John Mahaffey
> Dave Marr
> Bruce Lietzke
> Phil Rodgers
> Fuzzy Zoeller
> Fred Couples

9. Who was "The Silver Scot" whose grandson now is on Tour?

10. What woman holds the record for winning at least one tournament each year for 13 consecutive years?

> a. JoAnne Carner
> b. Amy Alcott
> c. Nancy Lopez
> d. Kathy Whitworth

11. What PGA star is Bob Goalby's nephew?

On the first tee of a medal tournament, Ronnie addresses the ball and begins his swing. As he starts downward, a gust of wind blows the ball off of the tee. Ron checks his downswing before it reaches where the ball would have been. Ruling, please.

There is no stroke. Ronnie successfully checked his swing under the 1989 Rule change. He may re-tee and play the shot with no penalty.

---

12. Who is the only player in history to hole a sand shot on the last hole to win a major tournament?

13. Fill in the blank. The top _____ players on the PGA Tour money list are exempt from having to qualify for their Tour cards.

    a. 100
    b. 125
    c. 175
    d. 200

14. Since 1980, when this record began, five of the players who have won the distinction of being the longest driver on Tour also share another distinction. Name it.

15. What pair of brothers teamed together to win the 1980 Disney World Team Championship?

16. Who is called "Mr. X"?

17. Who is the only Tour pro to ace the same hole in back to back rounds?

18. Two unrelated pros grew up in the town of Horseheads, New York. Name them.

Lou's ball comes to rest between two roots of a large tree. He cannot take a swing without possibly injuring himself or damaging his club. He places his sand wedge directly behind the ball and simply lifts it out in a hockey-type motion. Is this legal?

Lou's hockey-type stroke does not conform to the definition of a golf stroke. This is a two-stroke penalty or loss of hole in match play.

19. True-False. It was not until 1988 that a player won over one million dollars on Tour in one year.

20. Ben Hogan's first name is really not Ben. What is it?

21. What is the Vare Trophy given for?

22. Ben Crenshaw has won over four million dollars on the PGA Tour. How many majors has he won?

23. In 1957, the PGA Tour started its Rookie of the Year Award. Who was the first winner?

    a. Arnold Palmer
    b. Don January
    c. Paul Harney
    d. Ken Venturi

24. Who was called, "The pro from the moon"?

25. Who was the LPGA's first president?

26. What LPGA star was the first to earn over two million dollars in career prize money?

    a. Pat Bradley
    b. JoAnne Carner
    c. Amy Alcott
    d. Nancy Lopez

27. As of 1992, Tom Kite is the all time leading money winner on the PGA Tour. How many majors has he won?

28. Who was known as "The Hawk"?

29. Who is the all-time leading money winner on the LPGA Tour?

    a. Kathy Whitworth
    b. JoAnne Carner
    c. Nancy Lopez
    d. Pat Bradley

In a medal tournament, Gary lies two next to the green. He chips the ball but his club strikes the ball a second time while it is in the air. The ball goes into the hole. What is Gary's score for the hole?

Gary's score is four. Both times he touched the ball must be counted.

30. Who was the only player on the PGA Tour to be the leading money winner in the 1980s three times?
    a. Tom Watson
    b. Greg Norman
    c. Curtis Strange
    d. Paul Azinger

31. Can you name the player who won a PGA tournament in his 28th year on the circuit?

32. Name the touring pro who putts by grasping his left forearm with his right hand.

33. Who is known as "Mr. 59"? Who recently tied him?

34. True-False. Before going on the PGA Tour, players must present a financial statement to prove that they can support themselves on the Tour.

35. What company gave a free life insurance policy to any pro who would wear the company's name on his/her hat?

36. In order to make the LPGA Hall of Fame without winning a major, how many tournaments must a woman pro win?

37. Name the PGA Tour star and U.S. Open champ who was an All Big Eight defensive back in football for Colorado?

Kerry's ball has landed in a swiftly moving stream that has been marked as a lateral water hazard. She elects to play the ball out of the water. As she is making her swing the ball is moved by the rushing water. Nevertheless, she makes contact and the ball flies onto the fairway. Is this legal?

There is no penalty. The Rules allow for a ball to be played from running water.

38. Name the woman who won 13 LPGA victories in one year.
    a. Kathy Whitworth
    b. Patty Berg
    c. Mickey Wright
    d. JoAnne Carner

39. What pro is known as "Brillo" because of his hair?

40. What two time U.S. and Wimbleton tennis champion became a regular on the LPGA Tour?

41. Name the four tournaments on the LPGA Tour that are considered the majors.

42. What item of clothing is forbidden on the PGA Tour?

43. Who is the all-time leader in tournament wins on the LPGA Tour?
    a. Louise Suggs
    b. Mickey Wright
    c. Kathy Whitworth
    d. Betsy Rawls

44. Jack Nicklaus is one of two men to win the PGA Championship five times. Who is the other?

45. In the 1980s Jack Nicklaus won three of the four majors. Which one escaped him?

46. From 1971 to 1976, Jack Nicklaus was the leading money winner five out of these six years. Who was the only player to interrupt his streak?

47. Name the only woman to win the DuMaurier Classic three times.

48. What LPGA star has won the most majors?

    a. Mickey Wright
    b. Nancy Lopez
    c. Patty Berg
    d. JoAnne Carner

49. Who won the first three Walt Disney Opens?

50. This pro was almost crippled in an auto accident. Ben Hogan gave him encouragement to keep playing. A few years later he went on to win the PGA Championship with the lowest score in the tournament's history. Name him.

Nick and Gino are partners in a fourball match. Nick is forty feet from the cup and off of the green. He putts the ball and it starts right for the hole. Gino runs up to the flagstick and pulls it out just as the ball drops into the hole to win the match. The opponents cry foul.

Nick and Gino lose the hole. Rule 17-1 states that the flagstick must be attended before the shot is being played.

51. Who is the only player to win the Tournament of Champions three consecutive years?

    a. Arnold Palmer
    b. Jack Nicklaus
    c. Gene Littler
    d. Frank Beard

52. Only two players have won both the PGA and Senior PGA Tournament of Champions. Name them.

53. True-False. The players receive appearance fees for playing in PGA Tour events.

54. From 1978 to 1991, only three Americans have won a British Open Championship. Name them.

55. What 1980 U.S. Amateur Champ won the PGA Championship just three years later?

56. True-False. There has never been a back-to-back winner of the LPGA Championship.

Ski's five iron to the 18th hole is heading directly for the pin. Suddenly, a dog runs out and onto the green. The ball bounces off of the dog and out-of-bounds. Ski wants a ruling.

Sorry, Ski, due to a "rub of the green," the ball is out-of-bounds.

---

57. Who is the only player to win four consecutive PGA Player of the Year Awards?

    a. Tom Watson
    b. Arnold Palmer
    c. Jack Nicklaus
    d. Sam Snead

58. Name the Senior Star who won the Bob Jones Award, the USGA's highest honor.

59. What pro set a record by finishing in the money for 113 consecutive tournaments?

60. Out of these players who has won the most tournaments on the PGA Tour?

    a. Gary Player
    b. Lee Trevino
    c. Johnny Miller
    d. Ray Floyd

61. When Liselotte Neumann won the 1988 U.S. Women's Open, she set a tournament record with her 277. Whose record did she break?

62. True-False. Nancy Lopez has never won a U.S. Women's Open.

63. As of 1992, who of the following is not among the top ten all-time money winners on the PGA Tour?

    a. Lanny Wadkins
    b. Tom Watson
    c. Payne Stewart
    d. Lee Trevino

64. Who is the tallest player ever on the PGA Tour?

    a. Steve Jones
    b. Phil Blackmar
    c. Jim Dent
    d. George Bayer

65. Who are the only two men to win the PGA Seniors Championship and the USGA Senior Open in the same year?

While playing in a fourball match, Mike chips to within three inches of the cup. Tom, his partner, who has a tricky chip from off of the green asks Mike to leave his ball there. An opponent concedes Mike's putt. What should Mike do?

Mike has to pick the ball up.

66. Payne Stewart set a PGA record in 1988 by winning $553,571. What record did he set?

67. Who was the first leading money winner on the LPGA Tour starting in 1948?
    a. Jackie Pung
    b. Betsy Rawls
    c. Babe Zaharias
    d. Louise Suggs

68. Who was the first foreign player to lead the LPGA on the money list?

69. True-False. Scott Verplank won the 1985 Western Open as an amateur but he has never won a tournament as a pro.

70. In 1988, Sandy Lyle won the Masters one week after winning this tournament.
    a. The Buick Open
    b. The Heritage Classic
    c. K-Mart Greater Greensboro Open
    d. The Northern Telecom Open

71. The lowest score for nine holes in a PGA event is 27. Who holds this record?

72. Whose record of 11 consecutive PGA Tour wins is considered a record that could stand for all time?

73. Name the player who won an LPGA Tournament at the age of 18 to set a record?

    a. Nancy Lopez
    b. Marlene Hagge
    c. Betsy Rawls
    d. Pat Bradley

74. Name the only three players who have won back to back British Opens since 1960.

75. What current PGA star's father was a major league baseball star?

76. What number did PGA Senior pro John Brodie wear as a San Francisco 49er?

77. What college did Canadian pro Dave Barr attend?

    a. University of Ottawa
    b. Houston
    c. University of Washington
    d. Oral Roberts

78. What current Touring pro is a Doctor of Optometry?

In a match, Arthur is in a deep greenside bunker and cannot see the flagstick. He asks his partner to stand near the hole and hold up the flagstick so that he can see it while he plays his shot. Is this OK?

Yes, this is legal.

So You Think You Know Golf?

79. Where are the LPGA Headquarters located?

80. What LPGA rookie won three tournaments in 1988?

81. Who is known as "Sarge" on the Senior Tour?

82. What year did Jack Nicklaus join the PGA Tour?
    a. 1960
    b. 1962
    c. 1964
    d. 1966

83. What player went from 4th on the 1987 PGA Tour money list to 104th in 1988?
    a. Gary Hallberg
    b. Jack Nicklaus
    c. Scott Simpson
    d. Craig Stadler

84. What pro holds the record by finishing a tournament with five consecutive birdies?

85. What pro has won the same tournament eight times?

86. Who is "The Walrus" on the PGA Tour?

87. When the Europeans shocked the Americans in the 1987 Ryder Cup, who was the United States' captain?

Arnold's drive lands in a pile of soil in an area marked, "Under Repair." Arnold and his playing partners saw the ball fly into the pile of soil but they cannot find it. Ruling, please.

There is no penalty as this is "Ground Under Repair."

Corrine's ball is on the green. As she places her marker behind the ball to lift it, her hand strikes the ball and sends it rolling across the green. Is there any penalty?

Corrine must replace the ball to its original spot.

88. What PGA Senior Tour star spent most of his life as a steel worker?

89. What did all of the winners of the U.S. Women's Open from 1985 to 1988 all have in common?

90. Fay Crocker became the first foreign born player to win the U.S. Women's Open. What country was she from?

91. What pro won the PGA Championship the last year it was held before World War I (1916) then came back to win it again when it resumed in 1919?

92. For what is the Byron Nelson Award given?

93. What PGA pro was voted as having the best swing by his fellow competitors?

94. Who is the oldest player to win a PGA Tour event?
    a. Jack Nicklaus
    b. Sam Snead
    c. Ray Floyd
    d. Hale Irwin

95. What woman was the fastest to reach a million dollars in prize money on the LPGA Tour?
    a. Pat Bradley
    b. Patty Sheehan
    c. Beth Daniel
    d. Nancy Lopez

So You Think You Know Golf?

FOLLOWING THE SUN

THE
PROFESSIONALS

1. Tom Watson

2. Tom Watson led the PGA Tour from 1977 to 1980.

3. c. Billy Casper

4. Walter Hagen

5. It's awarded for the best stroke average for the season.

6. Jack Nicklaus has been runner-up 58 times.

7. Arnold Palmer

8. All are graduates of the University of Houston.

9. Tommy Armour

10. b. Amy Alcott

11. Jay Haas

12. Bob Tway holed a shot from the sand to win the 1986 PGA Championship.

13. b. 125

14. They lost their Tour cards.

15. Dave and Danny Edwards

16. Miller Barber

17. Arnold Palmer aced the 7th hole of the 1986 Chrysler Classic on consecutive rounds.

18. Mike Hulbert and Joey Sindelar

19. True. Curtis Strange earned $1,147,644 to set the mark.

20. William

21. Lowest stroke average for the season on the LPGA Tour

22. One—Ben's only major came in the 1984 Masters.

23. d. Ken Venturi

24. Kermit Zarley

25. Patty Berg

26. a. Pat Bradley

27. Tom Kite has won one major going into 1992.

28. Ben Hogan

29. d. Pat Bradley

30. c. Curtis Strange

31. Sam Snead won the 1965 Greater Greensboro, 28 years after his rookie year in 1937.

32. Bernhard Langer

33. Al Geiberger is known as "Mr. 59," but Chip Beck made a 59 in 1991.

34. True

35. Amana

36. Without winning a major, an LPGA pro would have to win 40 tournaments.

37. Hale Irwin

38. c. Mickey Wright in 1963

39. Bob Tway

40. Althea Gibson

41. The U.S. Women's Open, The LPGA Championship, The Dinah Shore, The Du Maurier Classic

42. Bermuda shorts

43. c. Kathy Whitworth has 88 wins.

44. Walter Hagen—1921, 1924, 1925, 1926, 1927
    Jack Nicklaus—1963, 1971, 1973, 1975, 1980

45. Jack did not win the British Open in the 1980s. He won the PGA and U.S. Open in 1980 and the Masters in 1986.

46. Johnny Miller was the big winner in 1974.

47. Pat Bradley

48. Jack Nicklaus

49. Bobby Nichols won the 1964 PGA with a 271.

50. c. Gene Littler—1955, 1956, 1957

51. Don January and Al Geiberger

52. False—this practice has been outlawed by the PGA.

53. Tom Watson, Bill Rogers and Mark Calcavecchia

54. Hal Sutton

55. a. Mickey Wright (8)

56. False. Micky Wright did it in 1960-1961, and Patty Sheehan did it in 1983-1984.

57. Chi Chi Rodriquez

58. Byron Nelson

59. b. Lee Trevino leads this group with 27 wins.

60. Neumann broke Pat Bradley's record of 279 set at La Grange Country Club in 1981.

61. True.

62. d. Lee Trevino

63. b. Phil Blackmar at 6'7"

64. Gary Player won both in 1988. Jack Nicklaus won both in 1991.

65. Payne set a record for the most prize money ever won without winning a tournament.

66. c. Babe Zaharias won $3,400 that year.

67. Ayako Okomoto of Japan

68. False—in 1988, Scott won The Buick Open as a pro.

69. c. The K-Mart Greter Greensboro Open

70. Mike Souchack in the 1955 Texas Open and Andy North in the 1975 BC Open

71. Byron Nelson

72. b. Marlene Hagge won the 1952 Sarasota Open at age 18.

73. Arnold Palmer 1961-1962
    Lee Trevino 1971-1972
    Tom Watson 1982-1983

74. Chris Perry's dad is Jim Perry, a major league pitching star.

75. 12

76. d. Oral Roberts

77. Dr. Gil Morgan

79. Sugar Land, Texas

80. Laura Davies from England broke in with three victories as a rookie.

81. Career army man Orville Moody

82. b. 1962

83. c. Scott Simpson

84. Jack Nicklaus finished the 1978 Jackie Gleason Inverrary Classic with 5 straight birds to win.

85. Sam Snead has won The Greater Greensboro Open 8 times—1938, 1946, 1949, 1950, 1955, 1956, 1960, 1965.

86. Craig Stadler

87. Jack Nicklaus

88. Walt Zembriski

89. For all of these women it was their first time winning an LPGA Tournament. Kathy Baker won in 1985, Jane Geddes in 1986, Laura Davies in 1987 and Liselotte Neumann in 1988.

90. Fay Crocker was from Uruguay.

91. Jim Barnes

92. Appropriately, this award is given for the most victories on the Tour that year.

93. Tom Purtzer

94. b. Sam Snead was 52 when he won the 1965 Greater Greensboro Open.

95. b. Patty Sheehan

9

THE JEWEL IN THE CROWN

THE U.S. OPEN

Ted and Larry are playing a match. Both players are on the green. While lining up his putt, Ted accidentally trips over Larry's ball and knocks it a few feet closer to the hole. Ruling, please.

Ted loses the hole, according to Rule 18-3b.

1. What is the lowest 72 hole score in Open history? Who did it?

2. What was the highest opening round by a winner?

3. What Open winner was a municipal club pro at the time of his win?

4. What player won the U.S. Amateur, then went on to win the U.S. Open the next year?
    a. Arnold Palmer
    b. Lanny Wadkins
    c. Jack Nicklaus
    d. Tom Watson

5. Who was the last player to win a U.S. Open in his first attempt?

6. What all-time great has been plagued with the tag "...but he's never won an Open"?

7. Who holds the record for the lowest score on a finishing round?
    a. Jack Nicklaus
    b. Tom Watson
    c. Hale Irwin
    d. Johnny Miller

8. Who won the Masters as a result of Roberto De Vincenzo signing an incorrect scorecard?

George smacks his drive off the first tee. The ball splits into two pieces. What can George do?

George may replay the shot with no penalty.

9. Who did Curtis Strange defeat in the 1988 U.S. Open playoff at The Country Club?
    a. Nick Price
    b. Nick Faldo
    c. Mike Nicolette
    d. Jack Nicklaus

10. How many times has Arnold Palmer won the U.S. Open?
    a. 1
    b. 2
    c. 3
    d. 4

11. Where was the first U.S. Open played?
    a. Chicago Country Club
    b. St. Andrews (New York)
    c. Newport Golf Club
    d. The Country Club

12. Who was the first player in Open history not to go over par in any of the four rounds?
    a. Lee Trevino
    b. Ralph Guldahl
    c. Jack Nicklaus
    d. Bobby Jones

13. True-False. Seve Ballesteros has never won a U.S. Open.

14. Name the two famous pros who lost the 1913 U.S. Open playoff to the young amateur, Francis Ouimet.

15. True-False. The U.S. Open is the only major to have an 18-hole playoff in case of a tie at the end of 72 holes.

16. True-False. Andy North has won more U. S. Open titles than Arnold Palmer.

17. Who came from seven shots back on the last day to win the 1960 Open?
    a. Jack Nicklaus
    b. Arnold Palmer
    c. Gary Player
    d. Billy Casper

18. In the 1950 U.S. Open, Ben Hogan returned from a devastating automobile accident to win the title in a three way playoff. Who were the two players that he defeated?

19. Who are the only two men to win the U.S. Open and the Canadian Open in the same year?

20. In 1938, a player made a 19 on the 16th hole of the final round at Cherry Hills. At the time he was just two shots behind the lead. Name him.

21. Three players hold the record for the lowest round (63) in a U.S. Open. Name them.

22. What was the name of the tournament that substituted for the U.S. Open during World War II?

Roger's putt ends up overhanging the hole. After walking up to it he waits for one full minute after which the ball finally tumbles into the hole. Is this legal?

There is a one stroke penalty. After walking to the hole he may only wait 10 seconds.

So You Think You Know Golf?

23. Who was the first four-time winner of the U.S. Open?

    a. Jack Nicklaus
    b. Bobby Jones
    c. Willie Anderson
    d. John McDemott

24. Who was the last player to win back-to-back Opens?

    a. Jack Nicklaus
    b. Tom Watson
    c. Curtis Strange
    d. Lee Trevino

25. Who was the last man to beat Bobby Jones in a U.S. Open?

26. Who is the oldest player to win the U.S. Open?

27. Who was the first American-born winner of the U.S. Open?

    a. Bobby Jones
    b. Francis Ouimet
    c. John McDermott
    d. Willie Smith

28. Two courses have hosted the U.S. Open six times each. Name them.

Herb carries binoculars in his golf cart and uses them to sight in on the pin placements. The binoculars do not measure distance and Herb argues that they are not an artificial aid any more than eyeglasses are. Ruling, please.

This is legal. The binoculars do not assist in gauging distance or help alignment.

---

29. What U.S. Open champ listed himself as "unattached" in the official list of club affiliation when he won?

    a. Bobby Jones
    b. Jack Fleck
    c. Lee Trevino
    d. Ralph Guldahl

30. Where did Tom Watson win his only Open?

31. In the 1939 U.S. Open playoff, Byron Nelson made an eagle two on the 460 yard fourth hole at Spring Hill on his way to victory. Who was his opponent?

32. Who was the last man to win the U.S Open and British Open in the same year?

    a. Jack Nicklaus
    b. Lee Trevino
    c. Tom Watson
    d. Ben Hogan

33. In 1969, an unknown pro, just out of the army, shocked the world by winning the U.S. Open at Champions. Name him.

34. Name the four U.S. Open Courses that have "Hills" in their names.

Charlie duck hooks his drive toward an out-of-bounds area. He plays a provisional and dubs it a few feet off the tee. He then hits his provisional ball onto the green. When walking down the fairway, Charlie finds that his first ball is in-bounds. What can he do?

Charlie may play his original shot since he did not play a shot beyond the original one.

81st U.S. OPEN CHAMPIONSHIP

HOLE	1	2	3	4	5	6	7	8	9	10	11	12	13	14	15	16	17	18
LEADERS PAR	4	5	3	5	4	4	4	4	3	4	4	4	3	4	4	4	3	4
BURNS	7	7	7	6	6	6	6	6	6	5	5	5	5	5				
GRAHAM D	5	6	6	6	5	5	5	5	5	5	5	5	5	6				
ROGERS	3	3	3	3	3	2	2	3	4	3	3	4	4	4	4			
RODRIGUEZ	2	2	2	3	2	1	0	1	1	1	0	1	0	0	0			
THORPE	1	1	1	1	1	0	0	0	1	1	1	2	2	2	2	1		
NICKLAUS	2	2	1	1	2	3	2	2	3	3	3	2	2	2	2			
CRENSHAW	2	2	2	2	2	2	2	1	1	2	1	1	1	1	0	0		
CONNER	1	0	0	1	0	1	1	0	0						0			
COOK J	1	1	1	1	1	1												
SCHROEDER J	2	2	1	1	0	0	0	0	1									

35. Name the four men who have won the U.S. Open four times each.

36. True-False. Tommy Armour never won a U.S. Open.

37. Who was the first player to win a U.S. Open who was neither American nor British?

38. Of the top 20 players on the 1991 Tour leading money list, how many have won U.S. Opens?

    a. 0
    b. 1
    c. 5
    d. 7

39. True-False. The prize money for the U.S. Open usually exceeds that of the British Open.

40. On what course did Ken Venturi struggle home with heat exhaustion to win the Open Championship in 1964?

    a. Winged Foot
    b. Medinah
    c. Seminole
    d. The Congressional

THE JEWEL IN THE CROWN

THE U.S. OPEN

1. Jack Nicklaus fired a 272 at Baltusrol in 1980.

2. 76—by Ben Hogan in 1951 and Jack Fleck in 1955

3. Jack Fleck

4. c. Jack Nicklaus

5. Francis Ouimet

6. Sam Snead

7. d. Johnny Miller

8. Bob Goalby

9. b. Nick Faldo

10. a. 1

11. c. Newport Golf Club

12. b. Ralph Guldahl

13. True

14. Ted Ray and Harry Vardon

15. True

16. True. He won in 1978 and 1985.

17. b. Arnold Palmer (Who else?!)

18. George Fazio and Lloyd Mangrum

19. Tommy Armour and Lee Trevino

20. Ray Ainsley

21. Johnny Miller, Jack Nicklaus and Tom Weiskoff

22. The Hale America Open

23. c. Willie Anderson

24. c. Curtis Strange (1988-1989)

25. Johnny Farrell in 1928

26. Hale Irwin in 1990 at the age of 45

27. c. John McDermott

28. Baltusrol and Oakmont

29. d. Ralph Guldahl

30. Pebble Beach in 1982

31. Craig Wood

32. c. Tom Watson

33. Orville Moody

34. Shinnecock Hills, Cherry Hills, Oakland Hills, Southern Hills

35. Willie Anderson, Bobby Jones, Ben Hogan, Jack Nicklaus

36. False. Tommy won in 1927.

37. Gary Player (South Africa)

38. a. 0

39. False. The money prize for the British Open is usually higher.

40. d. The Congressional

10

THE MOST STUDIED MOVEMENT OF MAN

THE SWING

Wendy's ball is on the edge of a river bank. To prevent her from losing her balance and falling into the water, her playing partner holds her by the belt while she plays a successful shot. Is this legal?

Wendy is receiving assistance, a violation of Rule 14-2. This means a two-stroke penalty or loss of hole.

1. What is the most popular grip used on the PGA Tour?
    a. ten-finger
    b. interlocking
    c. overlapping
    d. cross-handed

2. What causes a shank?

3. What does "coming over the top" mean?

4. What is a "forward press"?

5. What move in the golf swing disappeared when shafts began to be made from steel instead of wood?

6. True-False. A player has addressed the ball when he has taken his stance and begun his backswing.

7. What is a "strong" grip?
    a. a too firm gripping of the club
    b. both hands turned toward the left (right-handed player)
    c. both hands turned toward the right (right-handed player)
    d. a ten-fingered grip

8. What principle of physics is used to explain how speed is generated in the golf swing?

9. At impact, where should your weight be moving toward?
    a. your back foot
    b. your front foot
    c. your toes
    d. your heels

10. Why do most players place their eyes directly over the ball when they putt?

11. What is a "reverse pivot"?

12. What is "laying off" in the golf swing?

13. How should downhill lies be played?
    a. toward your back foot
    b. toward your front foot
    c. in the middle of your stance
    d. with your eyes closed

14. How do you hit a "punch shot"?

15. What is the most common cause of a slice?

16. What is the most popular type of grip that players use while putting?

17. What is a "chilly dip"?

18. What is a "knock down" shot?

19. True-False. Most putts are missed because they are misread.

20. What is a "lag" putt?

21. How do you play a ball that is buried deeply in the sand?

22. What is the overall speed of the swing is called?

    a. rhythm
    b. tempo
    c. acceleration
    d. swing speed

23. What is a "closed" stance?

Bob has a severe downhill lie during a match. After taking his stance, he places the club behind the ball but does not touch the ground or the ball. Suddenly, the ball starts rolling down the hill. His opponent claims that Bob has lost the hole. Is he correct?

There is no penalty. Bob has not addressed the ball since he did not ground his club.

So You Think You Know Golf?

24. What is "casting"?

25. What is a "thin" lie?

      a. the score that you tell your wife you made
      b. a lie that is deep in rough
      c. a lie where there is very little grass underneath the ball
      d. a lie where the ball is sitting up nicely

26. What is a "flat" swing?

27. True-False. A shot with a driver does not have any backspin.

28. True-False. On a short iron shot, the club should reach its lowest point at impact.

29. What usually causes a "fat" shot (hitting behind the ball)?

30. What is meant by the "arc" of a swing?

Harold has a three-foot putt in a big medal tournament. He misses the putt, and in disgust throws his putter into a nearby pond. He then sends his caddie to the clubhouse to get a replacement putter. He plays the last two holes with the replacement putter. Is this legal?

This is a four-stroke penalty. The club was not made unfit for play under normal conditions.

THE MOST STUDIED MOVEMENT OF MAN

THE SWING

1. c. overlapping

2. A shank is usually caused by striking the ball on the hosel of the club instead of the clubface itself. Most shanks are caused by standing too close to the ball at address, moving your weight onto your toes at impact or having a swing plane that comes into the ball from too sharp an angle from the inside or outside.

3. Coming over the top means that the clubhead is moved outside of the intended target line. It usually starts by spinning off of your back foot.

4. A forward press is a slight move toward the target with the hands, feet or legs. The forward press serves to break the inertia so that a smooth takeaway can be made.

5. The pause at the top of the swing disappeared when shafts began to be made from steel. With whippy wooden shafts, players had to pause at the top of the swing to allow the clubhead to spring back to level.

6. False. He/she must ground the club (touch the ground with the club).

7. c. both hands turned toward the right (right-handed player)

8. centrifugal force

9. b. your front foot

10. The player is now able to sight directly down the target line.

11. A reverse pivot occurs when a player holds or shifts his weight onto the back foot at impact.

12. Laying off means pointing the club well to the left of the target at the top of the swing instead of directly at it.

13. a. toward your back foot

14. Choke down, play the ball back in your stance, use a three-quarter swing and keep your wrists firm through the shot.

15. The most common cause of a slice is hitting the ball with an inside-out swing path. By swinging from the outside-in, the ball spins laterally and thus—the Big Banana.

16. Most players use the reverse-overlap by placing the forefinger of the top hand over the fingers of the bottom hand.

17. A chilly dip is a stubbed chip shot.

18. A knock-down shot is much like a punch shot only it is usually played with a wedge or 9 iron. The swing is kept low from back to front—the ball is pinched from the ground, flies low and stops quickly.

19. False. Studies have shown that putts are mostly missed because they are mishit (ball does not strike sweet spot on putter).

20. A lag putt is one that is intended to stop near the hole—close enough for a sure two-putt green.

21. There are two methods: (1) Open the clubface of the sand wedge as wide as possible and strike the sand a few inches behind the ball with a very firm swing or; (2) Close the face of the club, pick it up abruptly and slam it into the sand just behind the ball. This will cause the ball to squirt out and run considerably.

22. b. tempo

23. A closed stance will have your front foot closer to the target line than your back foot. It tends to promote a draw or hook.

24. Casting is letting go with the wrists at the top of the swing.

25. c. A thin lie is one that has very little grass beneath the ball.

26. A flat swing is one in which the hands are very low (near shoulder level) at the top of the swing. The club will tend to point away from the target instead of directly at it, at the top as well.

27. False. In order for a ball to become airborne it must have some amount of backspin to provide lift.

28. False. The lowest point should be reached after impact. Strike the ball first, then hit the turf.

29. Fat shots are caused by letting go with the wrists at the top of the swing or leaving your weight on your back foot.

30. The arc of a swing refers to the path of the clubhead.

So You Think You Know Golf?